AN OUTLINE

OF THE

HISTORY OF RUSSIAN

FREEMASONRY

BY

BORIS TELEPNEF

Reprinted from " The Freemason."

LONDON, 1928.

Kessinger Publishing's Rare Reprints
Thousands of Scarce and Hard-to-Find Books!

AN OUTLINE OF THE HISTORY
OF RUSSIAN FREEMASONRY

By BORIS TELEPNEF.

1.—RUSSIAN FREEMASONRY IN THE 18TH CENTURY.

A TRADITION, generally believed, existed among Russian Masons of the 18th century that the great reformer himself, Emperor Peter I[1], introduced Freemasonry into Russia, but there is no reliable evidence confirming this suggestive tale. The first Masons in Russia were, however, those foreigners who came to Peter's new capital, encouraged and attracted by the Emperor's commercial policy; hence the probable origin of the legend.

In 1731 Captain John Phillips was appointed by the Grand Lodge of England Provincial Grand Master for Russia. This is the first reliable information concerning Russian Masonry, and is minuted by the Grand Lodge of England on the 24th June, 1731, in these terms :—

> Then the Grand Master and his general officers signed a Deputation for our Rt. Worshipful Brother John Phillips, Esquire, to be Grand Master of Free and Accepted Masons within the Empires of Russia and Germany, and Dominions and Territories thereunto belonging, and his health was drank, wishing prosperity to the Craft in those parts.

Captain Phillips' adherents in Russia were mostly foreigners, bold seamen and keen merchants, whom the great spirit of adventure had attracted into the newly-opened country.

---

[1]Born, 1672; died, 1725.

In 1740 the next Grand Master for Russia, General James Keith, was appointed by the Grand Lodge of England.

General Keith[2] was one of the most remarkable personalities of his time, described as " a hero whose knightly and human qualities presented a high ideal and example for imitation and attainment." His romantic attachment to the unfortunate cause of the Stuart Pretender to the English Throne made him for long years an exile in foreign countries. Keith left the mark of his brilliant talents and indomitable energy everywhere he went. He was recommended to the Russian Court by the King of Spain, Philip V, and attained in the Russian service the highest military honours as an army leader of genius and of admirable personal courage. Keith also proved to be a capable and kind administrator. He was appointed in 1740 by Empress Anna Governor of Ukraine, one of the richest Russian provinces, but in those days ruined by constant war and the passage of troops. When Keith had left this post, the Ukrainians presented a petition to the Government complaining bitterly of Keith's recall :— " Either Keith should never have been appointed our ruler or else should never have been recalled."

Perhaps the most dramatic episode of Keith's turbulent life was the graceful reception accorded in London, in 1740, by King George II to the former exile, then already a distinguished general and renowned leader of men. Driven from Russia by intrigues of some jealous courtiers, he joined Frederick the Great in his constant and difficult wars, became Field-Marshal and an intimate friend of the Prussian King-Mason. He died as he lived, fighting bravely amongst his fellow soldiers.

A born leader, Keith succeeded in attracting into the Lodges not only many distinguished foreigners, residing in Russia, but also a number of Russian noblemen. Thus he was considered by Russian Masons to have been the first real propagator of Russian Masonry. A memory of his Masonic activities was preserved in a Masonic song of the period :—

After him (Peter the Great) Keith, full of light, came to the Russians and, exalted by zeal, lit up the sacred fire. He erected the Temple of Wisdom (a Masonic Lodge), corrected our thoughts and hearts, and confirmed us in Brotherhood.

[2]Born, 1696; died, 1758.

After the impetus given by Keith, Masonry began to spread in Russian society. Several Russian diplomats were initiated during their sojourn abroad, among them the prominent statesman, Count Golovin. Accordingly, Lodges following different Masonic systems were formed; some worked the three " symbolic " degrees only, on the same lines as English Lodges; others worked in addition, " higher " degrees, derived partly from Germany but mostly from France; a Chapter imparting Knight-Templar grades of the German system of Strict Observance was established in St. Petersburg.

YELAGUIN.

During the first part of this period (1731-1770), when no authoritative Masonic organization was as yet attempted in Russia, Masonry did not play any serious rôle in the awakening Empire. Masonry was, however, gradually becoming a fashionable pastime. This position of the Craft is well illustrated by the first Masonic impressions of His Excellency Ivan Yelaguin', the future " Grand Master of all Russias."

Yelaguin belonged to an ancient family of Russian nobility, and for many years enjoyed the friendship and confidence of Empress Catherine the Great.' He possessed an inquisitive mind and an unquenchable thirst for knowledge of hidden rites and sciences; sometimes this insatiable curiosity and ardent desire to penetrate into the " Mysteries of Nature and Science " brought him into contact with strange adventurers (Cagliostro, for example). Yet he was not devoid of critical intelligence, and in the end always emerged from his peculiar investigations sane in mind and judgment, richer in experience, though on some occasions a little poorer in his purse.

Yelaguin himself related that he joined Masonry partly out of curiosity and partly out of vanity. He was attracted by the secrecy of Masonic proceedings and also by the hope of meeting high-standing Russian courtiers and statesmen. He even expected, then far from the summit of his career, to obtain the friendship and help of influential Masons for his worldly affairs. At first unable to perceive any other purpose in Masonry, he saw in its

---

[3]Born, 1725; died, 1794.
[4]Born, 1729; died, 1796.

ceremonies " incomprehensible objects, strange rituals,
actions nearly deprived of sense "; in Lodges he thought
to hear only " of unintelligible symbols and of catechisms
unrelated to reason." He soon began to disapprove of the
whole Society : everything therein seemed to him "nothing
else but a playful game of persons who liked to be amused
at the expense of the novice, sometimes in a manner un-
permissible and undecorous." According to him, Masons
of those days first " joked with demure countenance in
the open Lodge," and afterwards " howled in a discordant
way during the meal, some incomprehensible songs, drink-
ing immoderately good wines at their neighbours' expense—thus finishing the beginnings of a service dedicated
to Minerva by worship of Bacchus."[5]

Yelaguin's description of early Russian Lodges was
confirmed later by an official Government report, char-
acterising those Masonic gatherings as such which produced only " jokes and mischievousness."[6]

Towards the middle of the 18th century the great truths
inculcated by Masonry—belief in God and necessity of
moral self-improvement—began to be appreciated among
some of the most educated and advanced Russian Masons.
This attracted into the Lodges a number of talented representatives of the younger generation, belonging to the
upper classes of Russian society. According to another
official report, presented in 1756 to the then reigning
Empress Elizabeth concerning a Petersburg Lodge, the
latter consisted of 35 members; among them were
Sumarokov, a well-known writer; Prince Scherbatov, the
future historian; Mamonov, of literary fame, and other
young noblemen of high culture and ability. Such
prominent grandees as Prince Golitzyn and Prince
Troubetzkoy also figured on the members' list.

The growth of Russian Masonry was somewhat checked
by those suspicions which the secrecy of Masonic proceedings provoked in the minds of some Government officials
—an occurrence not unusual even nowadays ! " Under
Empress Elizabeth," narrates Böber, one of the most
learned Russian Brethren, " Masonry began to spread in
Russia, but its members were so frightened for themselves

[5]Yelaguin's Memoirs. Russian Archives, 1864. Vol. 1,
593-594.

[6]Pekarsky. Supplements, 127.

and their good work that they assembled only seldom and in complete concealment, not in ordinary places, sometimes in a garret of a large house remotely situated." Amusing verses of that time depicting some of the imaginings about Masonic ceremonies were preserved, and here is an example of such versifying :—

> In Masonic proceedings there is such a clause
> That wins ever in Lodges the devil's applause:
> With swords they chase poor candidates there and about,
> And the gatherings' end is a devilish bout.

The official inquiry of 1756 " into the masonic sect "—" as to what is its foundation, and who constitute its membership "—did not reveal anything dangerous; in fact, the inquirers discovered that the Masonic institution " was but the key to friendship and eternal Brotherhood." Masonry was allowed to continue, though under slight police supervision.

Gradually the Empress's attitude became more benevolent; Masonry spread and enjoyed under her sceptre " the completest tranquillity." The earliest known lodges of this period are the Lodge of Discretion, founded in 1750, and its Daughter-Lodge of the Polar Star.

PETER AND CATHERINE.

A further impetus to Russian Masonry was given by Emperor Peter III.[7] There are reasons to believe that Peter III. himself was a Mason. The emperor established a lodge at his residence, Oranienbaum, and presented the Petersburg Lodge of Constancy with a house. A lodge was formed among the Emperor's supporters and favourites; one of its members was Archdeacon Andrew, Chaplain of the famous Preobrajensky Guard Regiment. Thus, Peter III. became an open protector of Russian Masonry. Unfortunately, his reign and even his life were cut short through a palace revolution in support of his strong-willed and shrewd wife Catherine; by the dethronement of her husband and the exclusion of her son, she forcibly ascended the Russian throne in 1762 as Catherine II.

Contrary to Peter III., a strict disciplinarian and a great admirer of military and administrative qualities of the

---

[7] Born, 1728; died, 1762.

Prussian Mason-King, Frederick the Great, Catherine II., of loose morals and sceptical mind, lent a willing ear to French free-thinkers, forerunners of the French revolutionaries. It was an anxious period before the outbreak of the Revolution in France; in many respects those days seem to be similar to the present era. Philosophers with an atheistic bend of mind, politicians with a disbelief in existing forms of society and its traditions, dreamers of new truths and violent changes in the political and economical structure of Europe, appeared first in France and then spread their demoralizing ideas over the whole of the Continent. Subversive societies, scoffing at any moral discipline, fostering discontent, and aiming at a general political upheaval, threw out their dangerous nets far and wide. Safe in her Empire, remote from the revolutionary hot-bed, Catherine II., during the first period of her reign, failed to realise the perils of French scepticism and materialism; French ideas suited her rationalistic mind as well as French morals suited her own character and that of her courtiers.

It is remarkable that several future leaders of Russian Masonry, later well known for their religious and patriotic views, did not escape in their young days from the contagion of French ideas. Yelaguin was for some time "heartily fond of godless writers" and became "acquainted with atheists who by their sweet poison of eloquence captivated his heart." But, like Yelaguin, other masonic leaders of Russia, after a short period of doubt and aberration, were helped to the road of religion and patriotism by the stabilising and elevating influence of Masonic tenets. They gradually united their forces under the banner of Masonry to fight the enemies of the true Masonic doctrines of faith and loyalty—the French atheists and revolutionaries. Hence came that important and beneficial rôle which Masonry played in Russia during the long reign of Catherine II. Masonry became a moral bulwark against the onslaught of foreign disruptive strivings.

Although the moral influence of Russian Masonry was gathering strength, no comprehensive organisation of the movement was yet attempted.

In 1762 the Lodge of Happy Agreement was officially recognised by the Prussian Grand Lodge of the Three Globes.

About the year 1705 an original Masonic System of Russian origin began to flourish in St. Petersburg. This System, named after its founder, Melissino's[8] Rite, was a peculiar combination of Symbolic Masonry with Templar grades, on which were superimposed semi-Catholic Church ceremonies. It was imbued with vague mystical teachings, interspersed with Kabalistic and Alchemical notions. The Rite consisted of seven degrees, and the meetings of the highest adepts were held either in churches or in chapels especially consecrated for the purpose. "Spiritual Knighthood" was conferred in the seventh degree, and this, perhaps, was the germ from which, later on, J. A. Starck's[9] Rite of Clerical or Spiritual Masonry was developed.

In spite of Melissino's efforts, his gorgeous ceremonies and involved speculations in mystical doctrines did not have either a widespread or prolonged success; the movement practically died out, within 10 to 15 years. Neither did other "higher" grades attract Russian Brethren, who then were still content with the three Symbolic degrees, although some of their leaders, Yelaguin included, were constantly seeking to enlarge their Masonic knowledge and experience by acquiring additional grades and rituals.

ZINNENDORF'S SYSTEM.

Attempts at some organisation of Russian Masonry became noticeable towards 1770; two Masonic systems arose almost simultaneously, and both achieved a considerable success. One was known as Yelaguin's System and followed strictly the regular work of English Lodges; the other was Zinnendorf's[10] System, which had vestiges of "higher" Templar grades according to the practices of the Swedish Masonic Rite, but in reality was also concentrated more on the three Symbolic degrees. Both Systems, although differing in ritualistic details and views on "higher" grades, in fact pursued the same main object: moral improvement of their members according to the precepts taught in the three regular degrees. Russian

---

[8]Peter Melissino, a Rusisan General, of Greek extraction; born, 1726; died, 1797.

[9]Born, 1741; died, 1816.

[10]Joh. Wilh. Ellenberger, called von Zinnendorf, after being adopted by his uncle; born in 1731; died in 1782.

Masons of both Systems worked with zeal, shaping the rough ashlar, symbol of a sinful man, into the perfect or cubic stone, symbol of a regenerated man.

Ivan Yelaguin played an important part in this healthy development of Russian Masonry. After a period of Masonic ignorance and doubt, this gifted man, through steady work in lodges, discussions with experienced Masons and the study of all available Masonic rituals and writings, learnt to appreciate Masonry and its import : an example which could be well followed by many waver- ing young Masons of our days. Thanks to Yelaguin's indefatigable activities, the English System became dominant. Yelaguin and his followers considered that " for the true Masonic teaching, three degrees are sufficient." Yelaguin in those days refused to work any of the " higher " grades, " not even the fourth."[11]

A Russian Grand Lodge.

On the 12th March, 1771, Baron von Reichel, a former courtier in Brunswick, established at St. Petersburg the Lodge of Apollo, an event of some significance in the his- tory of Russian Masonry. Before leaving Germany, Reichel had received from Zinnendorf himself an injunc- tion " to do everything possible for the glory and the increase of the true Royal Order (i.e., Zinnendorf's own Rite) in the domains of the Russian Empire." Well aware of Yelaguin's influence, Zinnendorf addressed to him a personal letter, saying : " With the purpose of strengthen- ing as much as possible friendship and accord among your brethren, I have considered it my duty to inform you of the foundation of the Lodge of Apollo, and to recommend worthy Brother Reichel and also lodges which may be further established, to your protection, confidence, and benevolence." In spite of this effort, Zinnendorf did not succeed in attracting into the scheme His Excellency Ivan Yelaguin; on the contrary, it seems that Zinnendorf's designs on Russian Masons prompted Yelaguin to form a Russian Grand Lodge.

Accordingly the Grand Lodge of Russia was established and Yelaguin was appointed its Grand

---

[11]The so-called " Scottish " degree.

Master by the Grand Lodge of England. This appointment was minuted on the 28th February, 1772, by the Grand Lodge of England in these terms : " The Grand Secretary informed the Grand Lodge that the Grand Master had been pleased to appoint His Excellency John Yelaguin, Senator, Privy-Counsellor, Minister of the Cabinet, etc., to Her Imperial Majesty the Empress of Russia, and Knight of the Polish Order of the White Eagle, and of St. Stanislaus, to be Provincial Grand Master of the Empire of Russia."

Zinnendorf's adherents in Russia could not well compete with Yelaguin's flourishing and authoritative organisation, and the Lodge of Apollo suspended its work. Still Reichel, an honest and fervent Mason, persevered. On the 15th May, 1773, he founded the Lodge of Harpocrates. The majority of its members were Russians, and among them Prince Troubetzkoy. Reichel's newly created lodge applied to the Grand National Lodge in Berlin for recognition, but received a rebuke from the Grand Master, who very properly advised Reichel to direct his request " to the Very Worshipful Provincial Grand Master, His Excellency State-Counsellor, Yelaguin, or to the Grand Lodge in London." In spite of this difficult situation, the indomitable Reichel continued his work and succeeded in establishing, in 1774, five new lodges : Horus, Latona, and Nemesis, in St. Petersburg ; Isis, in Reval ; and Apollo, in Riga ; and the lodge of Apollo at St. Petersburg reopened its doors. In 1776 Prince Troubetzkoy and Reichel founded in Moscow the Lodge of Osiris ; it consisted exclusively of brethren who belonged to the highest Russian aristocracy ; this lodge was even surnamed " the Princely Lodge." Reichel's example shows how much a convinced and diligent Mason can achieve in the teeth of utmost difficulties.

Meanwhile, Yelaguin also continued to work with conspicuous success. In 1774 he opened in St. Petersburg the Lodges of Nine Muses, Urania, and Bellona ; in Moscow the Lodge of Clio ; a military lodge was formed among Russian troops in Moldavia.

THE TWO SYSTEMS UNITED.

A curious thing happened in 1776. Shortly before this date the persistent Reichel requested the Grand Lodge of

Sweden to recognise his lodges, but his ambassador received in reply the same advice to make such an application to Yelaguin. Reichel then actually applied himself to the Provincial Grand Master of Russia and succeeded in persuading the latter that his (Reichel's) System had further and valuable Masonic revelations, in addition to those communicated by the Grand Lodge of England. Yelaguin agreed to introduce Reichel's System into his lodges, and a pact was concluded between the two leaders. On the 3rd September, 1776, Yelaguin's and Reichel's lodges were united. Yelaguin remained the Grand Master of Russia, but lodges united under him were working Zinnendorf's Rite with its additional degrees. The United Provincial Grand Lodge of Russia now counted eighteen dependent lodges; several other lodges remained, however, outside this union.

Yelaguin appeared to be quite satisfied. In a letter dated 2nd October, 1776, addressed to the Grand National Lodge in Berlin, he expressed his happiness " to see in the whole of Russia one shepherd and one flock." Reichel was also pleased, and thought that Masonic unity was " a message of Astrea's golden time returning to Russia." It was, however, hardly conceivable, in spite of the two leaders' satisfaction, that such divergencies of view as formerly existed between Brethren of two different systems could be laid down so easily. Differences of opinion soon showed themselves. Many studious Brethren, dissatisfied with the Union, began to seek " true " Masonry elsewhere.

Dissensions and disagreements undermined even Reichel's great courage and moral strength; he left all active Masonic work, disillusioned in his endeavours to preserve harmony and unity among the Brethren. With the withdrawal of this fervent propagator of Zinnendorf's Rite, the latter ended its rôle in Russia. The death blow to this System was delivered by a circular letter addressed by the Provincial Grand Lodge of Berlin to several Russian Lodges, stating that " Zinnendorf was a deceiver and known as such to all good Brethren."

Reichel himself continued to practise Masonry together with a few devoted adepts. He was held in great esteem by Russian Masons, and in cases of doubt his advice was readily sought. To one of the most prominent Russian Masons, Novikov, he had occasion to give an admirable advice which might be well followed even at the present time.

Bewildered by the different Masonic grades and rites appearing in the Russia of those days with a kaleidoscopic rapidity, Novikov, with tears in his eyes, implored Reichel to enlighten his doubts. Novikov said, " I do not ask you to give me still higher grades, nor to explain Masonry to me, for I have decided to wait in patience, practising as far as it lies in my strength, morals, self-know-ledge, and self-correction, but I ask you to give me a token by which I could without fault distinguish true Masonry from the false one."

Reichel replied: " All Masonry having political aspects is false; and should you notice even a shadow of political connection or any conjugation of the words equality and freedom, consider such Masonry to be false."[12]

On his side, Yelaguin evidently experienced the same disappointment with the ultimate result of the attempted union, for he gradually reinstated the orthodox English System in his Lodges, and they continued to work peace-fully till 1784, in which year, of their own accord, they suspended work; they resumed their Masonic labours in 1786.

SWEDISH INFLUENCES.

Reichel's success, though passing, was due to the desire of " greater " Masonic knowledge among leading Rus-sian Brethren, and this movement did not die out with his disappearance from the arena of active Masonry. The taste for " higher " Masonic mysteries, once acquired, remained; three degrees did not satisfy as heretofore. Neither did Reichel's System seem to be complete, and some of the Russian Brethren naturally turned towards Sweden, from whence Reichel's patron, the peremptory and ardent Mason, Zinnendorf, had obtained the begin-nings of his particular System, which in reality was only an incomplete edition of the Swedish Rite. In 1775 a number of Russian Masons decided to apply to the leaders of Swedish Freemasonry for instruction in " higher " Masonic knowledge of which Sweden was reputed to be

[12]Longinov, 076.

c

the custodian. Prince Alexander Kurakin,[13] "a most accomplished and amiable gentleman," and the bosom friend of the heir-apparent, Grand Duke Paul, was chosen by them for this important mission.

In Prince Kurakin a resplendent courtier was combined with an acute business man and a first-class diplomat. His exterior emphasized the high importance of his rank in the Russian Empire. He was often called " the Prince of Brilliants," for he loved to adorn himself with a wonderful display of jewellery—brilliants sparkled on his buttons, shoes, and buckles. Yet he had quite a sound understanding of the value of money, and by managing his large estates with sagacity he was enabled to secure an enormous revenue. It was, however, the Prince's attractive disposition, not his worldly advantages and uncommon intelligence, which made him rightly popular among Masons ; one of the Prince's contemporaries gave him the following character : " His sweetness was respected by everybody and charmed everybody. He also possessed nobility of feeling, and was reserved and prudent in his conversation ; he was a constant and tender friend."

Prince Kurakin eloquently explained to the Swedish Brethren the desires and fruitless researches of Russian Masons. The Swedish chiefs appeared to be ready to assist the skilful Masonic leader in his task, and Karl, Duke of Sudermania, himself undertook to initiate the Russian envoy into some of the higher mysteries of the Swedish system ; this happened in December, 1776. Prince Kurakin was hailed by Swedish Masons as " the future restorer of the Masonic Order in Russia." Unfortunately, all this was combined with a highly inconvenient condition—an act of strict obedience of Russian Lodges to the Supreme Council of the Order in Sweden. Having signed this act (probably not without misgivings), Kurakin was granted by his new Swedish chiefs " a constitutional warrant for the establishment at St. Petersburg of a ruling Mother-Lodge of the Swedish System under the name of the Chapter Phœnix."

THE CHAPTER PHŒNIX.

In 1778 the Chapter Phœnix was founded in St. Petersburg ; it was known to Brethren of lower degrees as the

---

[13]Born, 1752 ; died, 1818.

Grand National Lodge of the Swedish System; in **1780** a governing Directory for the Lodges of this Union was established. The foresighted and prudent Prince Kurakin left the leading part in this organization to another prominent Russian Mason, Prince Gavril Gagarin.[14]

Prince Gagarin, the future Minister of Commerce, was a man of great intellect, but one who seemed to have two souls in one body. Sometimes he was engrossed in deep studies of mysticism, and, to all appearances, a true and zealous Mason. Sometimes he would give up all his time to the most realistic pursuits of commerce and finance and bother but little about exercising Masonic precepts. This curious duality of nature probably stood him in good turn, for, besides his studies and inner Masonic work, he did not forget the practical aspect of a Masonic organization.

Under Gagarin's guidance Swedish Masonry achieved a considerable success; fourteen Lodges accepted his authority.

Swedish Masonry was organized on a most autocratic pattern; the Grand Master, assisted by adepts of higher grades, whose ruling offices were kept secret from ordinary Brethren, was responsible to nobody but his Supreme Chiefs in Sweden, and a strict obedience to him was demanded from all Brethren. Swedish degrees and doctrines, as then introduced into Russia, presented a peculiar combination of the three usual degrees with Templar and Rosicrucian grades.

Each of these three factors—Symbolic Masonry, Templar Degrees, and the Mystical Christianity of the Rose and Cross—helped to shape the Swedish System, and each impregnated Swedish ceremonial with its respective tenets and ideals; Symbolic Masonry, with a striving for moral improvement of each individual Brother, their mutual friendship and Charity; Templar Degrees, with the lofty dogmas of the Divine Trinity, Incarnation, and Love; Rosicrucianism, with mystical studies and practices. Thence the general plan of the work to be performed by every Brother as traced out by Masonic chiefs of the Swedish System was in three stages:—

1. Moral self-improvement and practice of Brotherly Love, Relief and Truth.

---

[14]Deceased in 1807.

2. Strengthening of Christian ideals and virtues in oneself and the world around.

3. Mystical attainment of approach to Christ Himself through His Inner Church.

Ceremonies staged with great pomp and recalling the knightly splendour of mediæval times were worked.

The mysteries of the highest grades were not communicated to the Russian Brethren in spite of repeated applications to Stockholm. In consequence they grew disappointed in the Swedish chiefs and, moreover, their dependence on these foreign Masonic rulers proved to be highly inconvenient, and even dangerous. The Empress naturally looked with suspicion on the subservience of many influential Russian Lodges to Stockholm, and at last commanded Yelaguin to take measures to have Gagarin's Lodges closed. In 1781 Gagarin left St. Petersburg for Moscow, where he continued his Masonic work in secret. The rôle of Swedish Masonry, and also of St. Petersburg as the main centre and inspirer of Russian Masonry, was terminated. At this period the predominance in the direction of Russian Masonry passed into the hands of Brethren in Moscow, where had gathered several of the most learned Masonic leaders.

Gagarin's arrival at Moscow did not result in any great changes among the Masons of the ancient Russian capital. Four Lodges began to work his Rite, but others continued as heretofore, some following the English System, some working the Templar grades of the Strict Observance, imported from Germany, or adhering to different rites of " higher " degrees brought from the inventive France. One of the most prominent leaders of Moscow Masons was Prince N. Troubetzkoy, ruling Master of the Lodge of Osiris, but he did not succeed in imposing his authority on the majority of Moscow Lodges; neither unity nor any authoritative Masonic organization existed among Brethren of the Russian metropolis, and many Lodges were languishing.

Recognizing this unsatisfactory state of Masonic affairs, the more fervent Masons remembered one more of Reichel's admonitions : " If you want to study true Masonry, you must have a hidden Lodge, consisting of a very small number of members, but discreet and constant, and practise in secrecy." Accordingly, they founded a Lodge called " Harmony." The following

Moscow leaders were among its members: Prince N. Troubetzkoy, N. Novikov, M. Heraskov, I. Turgenev, A. Kutuzov, I. Lopuhin. Each of them, from the part they played in Russian Masonry, deserves a few separate words.

Prince Nicholas Troubetzkoy[15] belonged to an ancient family of ruling princes who had kept their independence from the central Russian Government till the beginning of the sixteenth century. This famous family had given to Russia a number of renowned warriors and brilliant administrators; its representatives were of considerable importance at the Imperial Court. Prince Nicholas occupied the honourable post of a Senator. He was also an able writer and translator into Russian of several foreign books.

Nicolas Novikov[16] was probably the most remarkable personality among the Masons of Moscow. In **1767** Catherine II. appointed a committee of extraordinary importance for the purpose of working out a draft of a new Criminal Code; the Empress gave an order to select " a few young noblemen of special abilities " as secretaries of this committtee. Novikov became one of the secretaries; he was presented and most graciously received by the Empress. The secretarial work on a committee with such a far-reaching task gave Novikov ample apportunity to study the social conditions of Russia and the methods of its rulers. In **1768** he began to edit a satirical journal, the *Humble Bee*. In this edition he fought fearlessly against the bribery and corruption of the Empress's officials, the cruelty of many serf-owners, then still existent in Russia, the loose morals of the Imperial Court, and the atheistic tendencies of upper classes, under the spell of fashionable French ideas. Novikov even dared to start a controversy with the periodical, *Hodge-Podge*, a semi-official organ of the Empress herself, who in it advocated benevolent tolerance towards human weaknesses and vices. As a result of this " impertinence " the *Humble Bee* was stopped.

In **1772** Novikov undertook a new edition, the *Painter*, considered to be the best Russian periodical of the eighteenth century; it continued the tendencies of the *Humble Bee* and was suppressed during the next year.

---

[15]Born, 1744; died, 1821.
[16]Born, 1744; died, 1818.

Nothing seemed to break Novikov's courage, and in 1774 he began to issue a new magazine, the *Purse*, which was especially directed against the materialistic ideas and easy-going morals of Russian society, influenced by the French example. As a contrast, Novikov, with great patriotism, presented the virtues, high ideals, and moral strength of the Russian culture and beliefs. At the same time he published a number of historical works with the intention of strengthening national self-consciousness, and giving a picture of the ideals and manners of the Old Russia, "great in spirit, adorned with simplicity." Owing to these works, Novikov was allowed to examine the State Archives. His next publication, the *Ancient Russian Library*, was subsidised by the Empress, who restored Novikov in her grace, since he had contented himself with depicting virtues without flagellating the vices of her Court.

In 1777 Novikov started the *St. Petersburg Learned Reports*. The purpose of this paper was twofold : (1) to bring about a rapprochement between learned circles in Russia and abroad ; (2) to make known to the public the services of Russian writers. A monthly magazine, the *Morning Light*, followed this edition ; all the profit from the *Morning Light* was destined to the establishment of new schools for the unenlightened Russian masses. In 1779 Novikov was offered the lease of the Moscow University printing plant and the editorship of the *Moscow Records*, the University's official paper. He accepted this offer and moved to Moscow. During three years of his management the printing plant issued more books than had been published during 24 years of its previous existence. The number of subscribers to the *Moscow Records* increased seven times.

Novikov did not limit his work to the University alone. Among his other creations was the Friendly Learned Society, which later amalgamated with the Printing Company, also established by Novikov and his friends.[17] This company had an original capital of 57,500 roubles ; its yearly income became 40,000 roubles ! When closed in 1791, it still possessed a stock of books valued at 700,000 roubles, in spite of enormous yearly sales. The company had a large selling organization, not only at Moscow but also in provincial towns and even in villages.

---

[17]In 1784.

Under Novikov's influence the number of book-selling shops in Moscow alone increased from two to twenty. The first lending library in Moscow was established by him. During 1787, the disastrous year of the great Russian famine, Novikov organized efficient help for the starving population, distributing both food and medicine on an unprecedented scale.

M. Heraskov,[18] also a Russian nobleman, was one of the best writers of his time. He produced a number of poems, odes, and essays. His epic poems, " Rossiada " and " Vladimir Regenerated," were inspired by an ardent patriotism. He edited several magazines, was curator of the Moscow University, and a favourite of the Empress.

I. Turgenev[19] belonged to Russian nobility, and was rector of the Moscow University; he was considered by his contemporaries, and justly so, to be " one of the most enlightened men of his time."

A. Kutusov[20], of a noble Russian family, at first served in the Russian Army, but inclined to the study of theoretical and practical mysticism, soon retired from all active service, and spent the remainder of his life engrossed in mystical and occult lore. He translated into Russian some of Paracelsus' works, Klopstock's " Messiah," Young's "Useful Thoughts," and many other writings of a similar character.

I. Lopuhin,[21] as was customary among members of the Russian nobility in those days, first entered military service; he retired with the rank of colonel. In 1782 Lopuhin was appointed Counsellor and, later, President of the Criminal Court of Appeal in Moscow; in this post of high responsibility he proved to be an impartial and strict judge, yet one who was always ready to soften the unnecessary cruelty of the Russian laws of his time. In 1785 Lopuhin left the Civil Service and devoted himself to literary and philanthropic activities. He translated many mystical writings, helped the poor in every possible way, organised schools, established printing plants at Moscow, and educated abroad at his own expense poor

[18]Born, 1733; died, 1807.
[19]Born, 1752; died, 1807.
[20]Died in 1790.
[21]Born, 1756; died, 1816.

Russian students. He wrote a number of important Masonic works, such as " The Moral Catechism of True Freemasons," "The Spiritual Knight or Seeker of Wisdom," etc. All his works were characterised by a Christian spirit, deep patriotism and loyalty to his National Sovereign and Church. Paul I. called Lopuhin to St. Petersburg and made him Secretary of the State and afterwards member of the criminal department of the Moscow Senate. Lopuhin was entrusted with missions of the highest importance and responsibility both by Paul I. and his successor, Alexander I.

These exceptional men, attracted by Masonry, which brought forth their best qualities and energies and united them, called their new Lodge of Harmony a "scientific " Lodge. They did not practise ritual in this particular Lodge; they studied, compared and collected Masonic knowledge. Evidently, a Lodge on the lines of the famous Quatuor Coronati Lodge in London was founded by these zealous Masons.

A German teacher, I. Schwartz,[22] became associated with the Lodge of Harmony. Initiated in Russia, his adopted country, he was a convinced Mason : "An indefatigable enthusiast, he was ever burning as if he were an inextinguishable fire, and he burnt himself to ashes in a life of 33 years." Schwartz proposed to the other members of the Harmony Lodge that he would travel to Courland, where he hoped to obtain an insight into "further Masonic mysteries " not known to Moscow Brethren. Accordingly, he arrived at Mittau, in Courland, in 1781. There he obtained two important letters of introduction : one to the celebrated Berlin mystic, Wöllner; and the other to the famous surgeon, Teden, who both played a prominent rôle in the Masonic Order of the Rosy and Golden Cross (first instituted in the south of Germany). For this help Schwartz had to promise his Courlandish friends to propagate in Russia the "Templar " grades. Schwartz well knew the inconvenience of this condition; several Russian Masons of high standing, among them the influential Novikov, disliked the pomp of "knightly " degrees, and, being Russian patriots, objected to a dependence upon a Grand

---

[22]Died in 1784.

Master residing abroad.[23] Nevertheless, carried away by the fervent desire to acquire deeper Masonic knowledge, Schwartz agreed.

He saw Wôllner in Berlin and was initiated into " a Rosicrucian grade." Soon after that, on the 1st October, 1781, Schwartz received from Teden a Warrant appointing him "the only Supreme Chief of the Theoretical Degree in the whole Russian Empire and its Dependencies." The Theoretical Degree was introductory to " Rosicrucian grades "; only those who had passed this degree could be admitted into the Rosicrucian Order itself. Schwartz, therefore, became the actual chief of all Russian Rosicrucians. To placate Novikov, Schwartz arranged for Novikov's appointment as Chief Warden of Russian Theoretical Brethren; at the same time Schwartz succeeded in obtaining from the Duke of Brunswick, the Grand Master of the Masonic Templar Order in Germany, a formal promise to support, at the next Masonic Congress, the Russian demand for independence or autonomy.

At the beginning of 1782, Schwartz came back. His weakness in acceding to the demand for propagation of Templar degrees in Russia was soon forgiven; leaders of Moscow Masons found the mystical teachings of the Rosicrucian Order a superstructure worthy of " true " Masonry, and were prepared to pay the price agreed, "for the great delight of being received into the embrace and blessing of the Order of the Rosy Cross."[24]

Here ended the search of Russian Masons for deeper Masonic mysteries—Christian mysticism,[25] as embodied in the Rosicrucian grades, so much in accord with the mystic ceremonies of the Russian Church and the inherent strivings of Slav character, satisfied them completely. From Schwartz's return to Moscow till his death Russian Masonry, concentrated chiefly at Moscow, had a double organisation : a Provincial Chapter and a Directory of the " Knightly grades," in reality the "outer " circle, from which the candidates were selected for advancement, and the "inner " circle, or the Order of the Rosy Cross.

---

[23]At that time the Grand Master of the Templar System of Strict Observance was Ferdinand, Duke of Brunswick—a *foreign* Prince.

[24]Not to be confused with the Rose-Croix degree, quite a different institution. Rosicrucians in Russia were often called "Martinists."

[25]Then fashionable in many parts of the European Continent.

In 1782, the Wilhelmsbad Masonic Congress, convoked by the Chiefs of the Strict Observance, was held. The Templar System of the Strict Observance was transformed into the Rite of Knights Beneficent of the Holy City and the Templar Origin of Freemasonry denied. The idea of a reconstituted Templar Order, heretofore embodied in the Strict Observance, was thus rejected, to the great joy of the Russian Brethren, and Russia was acknowledged an autonomous (8th) Province of the Reformed or "Rectified" Rite.

Gradually all "Knightly" degrees fell into disuse among the majority of Russian Masons, and the work of their Moscow leaders was centred entirely on the Rosicrucian Order. They severed their connexion with the Duke of Brunswick in 1783; the authority of Wöllner, the Supreme Berlin Chief, was in the end the only one recognized by them.

The activities of Russian Rosicrucians were remarkable and left deep traces in Russian literature and life. Under the leadership of Schwartz, Novikov and Masons of similar type, they fought valiantly, and often successfully, against atheism and loose morals; they upheld patriotic and sane traditions of the Russian State and Orthodox Church; they did their utmost to bring enlightenment and health to the uneducated masses. Rosicrucian ideals were propagated by means of periodicals founded and directed by their leaders, by the printing and translation of suitable books, by the establishment of schools and libraries. Their philanthropic work was unrivalled; they cured gratis in towns and villages; they helped in the most stricken regions during times of famine, and sacrificed entire fortunes in the cause of charity.

The doctrines inculcated by the Russian branch of the Rosicrucian Order can be thus summarized. For the basis of their teachings Rosicrucians had two great Masonic ideals—charity and self-improvement. To this firm foundation of three Masonic degrees were added Rosicrucian grades, the aim of which was to initiate worthy Brethren step by step into the mystical or "esoteric" Christianity, understood in the light of ancient and mediæval occult schools. The most vital problems of life —those of relationship with man, universe and God, redemption of man through Christ, hidden laws of Nature, etc.—were debated upon and diligently studied in their

Temples. Mystic union with God through Christ was the last step of their work of perfection—the "transmutation" of the base into the high. Among the Rosicrucians were, however, a few who strove to achieve this transmutation on the physical plane by endeavouring to "make gold" from base metals, and who also believed in the Universal Medicine; but these notions were not characteristic of the general Rosicrucian movement in Russia, rich in lofty teachings on the spiritual plane and in practical achievements on the social plane.

In February, 1784, Schwartz died. His death dismayed Moscow Rosicrucians, and was undoubtedly a great loss to the cause. His successor, Baron Schröder, appointed from Berlin, did not possess the high qualities of their deceased leader; he seemed to be an unsteady man, inclined to speculations and fantastic ideas, hardly worthy of the great responsibility thrust upon him by Teden.

In 1784 a "silanum" was proclaimed by the Rosicrucian Chiefs in Berlin, i.e. a period during which no new members could be admitted into the Order and the usual outward work was suspended. In spite of the "silanum," Russian Rosicrucans continued their studies and enlarged their influence in "the outer circle" by opening new Masonic Lodges. Rosicrucian influence was so strong that their doctrines penetrated even into Yelaguin's Lodges (which had resumed their work in 1786). Although not recognising and, in fact, disavowing the Rosicrucian Order, Yelaguin introduced into his reopened Lodges "higher" degrees impregnated with theories and doctrines similar to Rosicrucian teachings.

One of the reasons for the Rosicrucian "silanum" is not without interest. In those days, not unlike our own, great fears existed that subversive societies of revolutionary tendencies were endeavouring to sow corruption and discontent everywhere, even by penetrating into legitimate unions of the opposite camp.[26] Rosicrucians, who stood for the upholding of Monarchy and Religion, were bitter enemies of the revolutionary Illuminati.[27] To remove every

[26]Longinov, 082.

[27]Who are supposed to have survived their dissolution and to have played a pernicious rôle in the Central Europe till our days.

chance of revolutionary penetration into their Lodges, Rosicrucians proclaimed the said strict " silanum."

In 1785, full Rosicrucian activities were apparently again resumed in Russia. But clouds were gathering over their heads : already in 1786 the Empress Catherine began to view Rosicrucians with suspicion. The unfortunate dependence of Moscow Rosicrucians upon their Chiefs in Berlin was disagreeable to the Empress, an arch-enemy of Prussia; their association with the heir-apparent, Grand Duke Paul, an open adversary of Catherine II, seemed to her highly suspicious; criticisms of loose morals of the Imperial Court irritated her; their strict adherence to ancient Russian traditions and to the orthodox Church went against her temporary but strong leanings towards French ideas and customs and her sympathetic attitude to the Jesuits. Hence the Empress's animosity, at first expressed in her comedies ridiculing Masons and confounding them with charlatans and rogues; this literary way did not avail, and sterner measures had to be applied.

Investigations were made through the Moscow police, but nothing incriminating could be proved against the Rosicrucians. The Empress thought to enlist the concurrence of the Church, but did not succeed in this attempt either. Most of the Russian hierarchs, contrary to the Roman Clergy, looked without disfavour upon the Masonic movement, and Masons themselves considered their fundamental doctrines and the basis of their rituals to be identical with the practice of the Greco-Catholic Church of Russia.[28] Novikov was examined in the orthodoxy of his Christian beliefs by the high dignitary of the Russian Church, Archbishop Platon, and the latter reported to the Empress : " I pray to the all-merciful God that not only among the flock entrusted to me by God and you, most Gracious Empress, but all over the world there would be such Christians as Novikov."

Nevertheless, spurred on by the terrors of the French revolution and the general fear of every secret society, however beneficial, Catherine II forbade further Rosicrucian activities. Novikov was thrown into the dreary dungeons of the Schlusselburg fortress. The main point of accusation against Novikov was his growing popularity

---

[28]Eshevsky, III, 482.

among Russian society and his alleged close connection with the Grand Duke Paul. His admirable activities assumed in Catherine II's eyes, quite wrongly, a dangerous character as possibly paving a way for the Grand Duke's ascendancy, Novikov was a victim of a suspicion, "understandable but not justified." [29]

It must be borne in mind that the Empress's attitude towards Novikov did not represent her views on Masonry as such. Catherine II held Yelaguin's Lodges in high esteem. Although, for the reasons already explained, she decided to close the Masonic Lodges, she did not change her attitude towards their leaders; most of them retained their rank at the Court, their offices in the Government services and the Empress's favour.

According to the wish expressd by the Empress, in 1792 officially all Masonic Lodges in Russia were closed; Masonic work could be continued only in private meetings of devoted Brethren.

In 1796 the Grand Duke Paul ascended the Russian throne. The new Emperor, Paul I,[30] belonged himself to the Masonic Fraternity: a document, which was preserved in the Imperial Archives at the Russian Ministry of Police, stated quite unequivocally that Grand Duke Paul had been secretly initiated by I. P. Yelaguin. The Emperor's mentality was different from his mother's, the deceased Empress. During her life he was distinctly hostile to her idealogy and her Court. The Grand Duke was religious and inclined to mysticism, just the opposite of the sceptical mind of the old Empress; it is not surprising that he took interest in Masonry and particularly in Moscow Rosicrucians.

Most of the Emperor's faithful adherents during his difficult life before ascending the Russian throne were Masons. His teacher and intimate friend, Count Nikita Panin, a prominent statesman, was an earnest Mason. Prince Nicholas Repnin, one of the greatest generals of his time, was another friend of the Emperor's and also a zealous Mason. Prince G. Gagarin and Prince A. Kurakin were both Paul I's favourites. During his journey abroad the Grand Duke had met Frederick the Great and other well-known Prussian Masons; his reception by

---

[29] Karamsin's Memorandum (Longinov, 0162).
[30] Born, 1754; died, 1801.

them is said to have been extraordinarily friendly, and exceptional honours were accorded to Paul by the Prussian Court.

Unfortunately Paul I's abnormal and humiliating position during his mother's life was gradually spoiling his nature. He grew suspicious and irritable, even somewhat unbalanced.

As soon as he had acquired the Supreme Power in Russia, Paul I showed marks of high favour to Masons, and especially to those who had been under a cloud in the previous reign; Novikov was released immediately. Soon, however, the unfortunate ruler cooled considerably towards his Masonic friends, who bravely told the Monarch unadorned truths and gave him frank and honest advices. He decided to postpone the reopening of the Lodges; instead he visited an assembly of their leaders, and while all agreed to defer for a while the opening of Lodges, the Emperor shook hands with everyone and said: " If you want anything, write to me plainly as to a Brother, without any compliments."

The Emperor's interest in the Order of Malta, then a rival of Masonic " knightly " degrees, was probably the chief reason for his apparent neglect of Russian Masonry.

Though assured of the Emperor's benevolence, Russian Masons continued their work only in private gatherings and by individual practice and study.

II.—RUSSIAN FREEMASONRY IN THE 19th CENTURY.

In 1800, one of the leaders of the Rosicrucian Order, A. Labsin,[31] founded in St. Petersburg the Lodge of the Dying Sphinx and gathered in it a number of adherents to mystical doctrines and Rosicrucian pursuits. Rosicrucians were, however, extremely careful in the selection of their candidates. Also they were, and not without reason, suspicious of other Masonic systems, ever watchful not to admit any one connected with political or spurious Masonry, " a wolf in sheep's clothing." Although not organized like their predecessors, they carried on the same work of enlightenment and philanthropy. In 1803, Rosicrucians opened another secret Lodge in Moscow—" The Neptune."

In the meantime members of the Lodge of the Pelican, in St. Petersburg, were preserving the traditions and rituals of the Swedish System.

In addition to the uninterrupted activities of the Rosicrucians and a faint survival of the Swedish Rite, adherents of French grades also continued their work. A French lodge, " The United Friends," was opened at St. Petersburg, in 1802. Its object, following French freethinkers' ideas, differed both from the Rosicrucian and Swedish systems: it was " to remove distinction of races, classes, religions, principles; to exterminate fanaticism, prejudices; to destroy hatred among nations and to abolish wars, uniting the whole mankind in love and science." A very lofty ideal, but obviously containing a germ of a wide political programme, and therefore, hardly without danger for Masons! This Lodge united a section of the liberal Petersburg society and soon was looked upon with some misgivings by the Russian Authorities.

Such was the position of Russian Masonry when the Emperor Alexander I,[32] who at first regarded Masonry

---

[31]Born, 1776; died, 1825. Vice-President of the Imperial Academy of Arts.

[32]Born, 1777; died (under mysterious circumstances), 1825.

with ill favour, himself became an initiate and thus gave a powerful impetus to the full restoration of Russian Masonry. The history of Russian Masonry from this revival at the beginning of the 19th century till its subsequent dissolution can be divided into three periods.[33]

THE FIRST PERIOD.

The first period continued till about 1814.[34] It was characterized by the actual and official predominance of the Swedish System, supported by the Russian Government. The Leaders of Swedish Masonry in Russia were men of conservative, strictly Christian and highly nationalistic views. The Government, which kept vigilant watch over secret societies and their members, endeavoured to use Masonry as a sort of political department. To carry out such a plan the constitution of Swedish Masonry was admirably suited and could be easily adapted. Towards 1814, when officially this System was without rivals, no other Masonic rite being then tolerated by the Russian Government, Russian Masonry was in reality organized on the following lines :—

The autocratic Emperor of Russia.

The Ministry of Police, responsible to the Emperor.

The autocratic Ruler of Masonry[35]—Grand Master and Grand Prefect, not responsible to the Brethren but responsible to the Ministry of Police.

Two secret Councils of the adepts of " higher " Masonic degrees, dominated by the Grand Prefect.

The Grand Lodge, openly known and called " The Grand Directorial Lodge Vladimir to Order,'' entirely dominated by the Grand Master and his councillors of high degrees.

Ordinary Lodges.

---

[33] For fuller details, see A.Q.C., XXXVIII, Part I (Some Aspects of Russian Freemasonry during the Reign of Emperor Alexander I ").

[34] It is interesting to note that the national hero and liberator of the Russian Empire from the French invasion in 1812, Prince Kutusov, was a leader of Russian Masons.

[35] A zealous and studious Mason, I. Böber, filled this place; he is reported to have shown and convinced Alexander I of the high ideals and usefulness of Masonry.

This peculiarly constituted Masonry, controlled ultimately by the Ministry of Police and largely used for the support of the existing Russian Government, a highly laudable but purely political object, was certainly not the unadulterated Masonry as practised by Yelaguin's and the Rosicrucian Lodges of the 18th century, on the pattern of regular Lodges in England. The movement became, nevertheless, quite fashionable, and large numbers of new members began to swell its ranks. Unfortunately, no great discrimination was made among candidates, and many quite unworthy initiates were soon enjoying " Masonic privileges."

The Governmental interference and control drove into secrecy several Lodges and Chapters—some, because they could not bear the idea of Masonry being supervised or directed by one autocratic chief, himself under the control of the Ministry of Police; others, because it harboured members with views divergent from the Government, and, therefore, without any hope of obtaining the necessary permission for their meetings.

Among the first were the Rosicrucians, who preferred to work independently, guarding their ranks from undesirable members and all politics, of whatever kind; they persevered in the traditions of their predecessors, working the three regular Masonic degrees, supplementing their teachings with studies of Christian mysticism; they continued the editing of books and periodicals, and, also, the educational and philanthropic work.

In the authorized Lodges themselves all was not well. The rigid system just described and the political object underlying it gradually provoked a powerful opposition in the Masonic ranks. This began among Brethren of German origin and sentiments, who, not unnaturally, were dissatisfied with the extreme nationalistic views of Masonic leaders; they were then much influenced by two German Masonic Systems—Fessler's and Schröder's—both of which introduced a certain rationalism into Masonic teachings and denied the ruling position of any degree higher than that of a Master Mason. Consequently, German Brethren opposed the influence of the higher degrees of the Swedish System, also its nationalistic tendencies and strictly Christian character, tinged with mysticism in the highest grades. Politicians of Liberal and Radical opinions, who had been admitted into

" Swedish " Lodges in Russia rather indiscriminately, united around them as well. This opposition soon grew to such an extent that open disagreements arose in the Grand Directorial Lodge Vladimir.

THE SECOND PERIOD.

The increased influence of Rationalistic and Liberal tendencies, as expressed in the growing opposition to the acknowledged leaders of Swedish System in Russia, marks the beginning of *the second period* of Alexander I's Masonry, and can be assigned to 1814.

Disagreements in the Grand Directorial Lodge continued with a conspicuous lack of Brotherly love; the Ministry of Police itself was approached by the champions of two different currents of Masonic thought to enlist its sympathies and to induce it to support one side against another! The Ministry of Police, evidently disappointed in the usefulness of mutually antagonistic and quarrelling Masons, washed its hands of the whole matter and did not interfere. Grand Master Böber found it impossible to retain his troublesome office any longer, and resigned at the end of 1814. Count Shouvalov was elected to succeed him, but declined the honour.

At last Count V. Mussin-Poushkin-Bruce was installed as Grand Master. His sympathies were evidently on the side of the opposition; for he immediately allowed great changes in the established traditions and tendencies of the Grand Directorial Lodge. This naturally led to sharp controversies. Matters came to a definite crisis during the summer of 1815. A reconciliation between two camps appeared out of question. It was then decided to close the Grand Directorial Lodge Vladimir and to establish instead two Grand Lodges, equal in rights and independent of each other. The Ministry of Police was informed and raised no objection. Consequently, on the 30th August, 1816, four Lodges, adherents of the new tendencies, established the Grand Lodge Astrea.[36] Three other Lodges (of the seven which constituted the former Union) founded the Provincial Grand Lodge of the Swedish System.

---

[36]Some Brethren, followers of French Rites, played a not unimportant rôle in organizing the Astrea.

Hence, Liberal (and, in part, German) tendencies destroyed Masonic unity in Russia and became for some time dominating: whereas the conservative Provincial Grand Lodge languished, the other Grand Lodge steadily increased its membership. Again there was no due discretion used in selecting candidates for the Astrea's Union.

As a reaction against the rigidity of the Swedish System the Grand Lodge Astrea showed an amazing tolerance. True, only three symbolic degrees were officially recognized, but these degrees could be worked in a way every individual Lodge chose. Democratic in its essence, the new Grand Lodge extended its hospitality to many widely divergent Masonic Systems, to peculiar Rites and strange members, some of whom joined Masonry, quite frankly, for social advantages, some for jovial and others even for political reasons.

A shapeless agglomeration of men of different views, Russian Masonry of that period was drifting to certain peril. No wonder that the Rosicrucians still kept aloof; they worked steadily and quietly and were held in great esteem by the best Masons of the new formation.

THE THIRD PERIOD.

A weakened organization is open to all harmful influences; so Russian Masonry unsuspectingly opened its doors to elements more dangerous than Russian Liberals and Rationalistic German Brethren with their followers; it opened its doors, though unwittedly, to atheists and their near companions—revolutionaries. Thus began *the third period* of Masonic history in Alexander I's time.

It is difficult to determine with any precision when this happened; probably already in 1818 the character of membership of several Lodges was growing highly doubtful. As some Lodges included police officers and even *agents provocateurs*, the ultimate doom of Masonry in Russia was becoming evident. Political tendencies with revolutionary aims, which then animated a number of Brethren, were certainly known to the Government and viewed with disgust and alarm by loyal, true Masons and their old leaders. This was expressed in a remarkable document presented to the Emperor, Alexander I, by

Lieutenant-General and Senator Egor Kushelev,[37] Deputy Grand Master of Astrea in 1820 and the virtual ruler of its Union, elected to this honourable post by the unanimous consent of the Brethren. The Emperor received Kushelev's report in June, 1821. In this report Kushelev, appalled at the state of Masonic Lodges in Russia, implored the Emperor either to close them altogether or to reform them, introducing strict discipline and one central authority—in fact, he advocated the reinstatement in its old splendour of the Swedish System as formerly practised by the Grand Directorial Lodge Vladimir.

The vacillating mind of the Emperor did not seem to be able for some time to take a definite step against Lodges. His previous association with Masonry and a personal regard for many worthy Brethren and for the principles of the Institution might perhaps account for the delay. At last, on the 1st of August, 1822, the Emperor decreed the closing of all Masonic Lodges in Russia, and they were closed without any trouble, not to be opened officially during the remainder of the century.

The main reasons of this disaster were but too clear: first, lack of necessary discrimination when selecting new members; and, secondly, admission of politics, if only in a few Lodges. These reasons seem to operate in the same perilous way for Masonry in some countries in our own days!

It must be noted that Rosicrucian Lodges continued to work in secrecy and quiet; apparently they survived through the whole of the 19th century, carrying on the great traditions of the Masonic and Rosicrucian leaders of the brilliant period of Russian Masonry during Empress Catherine II's reign.

Alexander I's decree was confirmed by his successor, Nicholas I, on the 21st of April, 1826.

In spite of the dissolution, besides the aforesaid Rosicrucian activities, private Masonic gatherings worked old rituals, continued Masonic studies, and even initiated new members; they are well depicted in a Russian novel of the 19th century, " The Masons," by Pissemsky.[38]

---

[37]Born, 1763; died, 1826.

[38]There are some interesting sidelights on Russian Masonry of the 19th century also in Tolstoy's celebrated novel, " War and Peace."

Police supervision became, however, very strict, and these activities weakened considerably, only a few isolated Masons still practising the Royal Art in the seclusion of their private studies.

Unfortunately, other secret organizations under the respectable cloak of Masonry made their appearance in Russia from time to time, pursuing exclusively political aims, often of a pernicious kind. This circumstance, coupled with the political aspect which took some of the Masonic bodies on the Continent, especially in the Latin countries, gradually turned the Russian Government and Society against *all* Masonry, however orthodox and beneficial for the State; in fact, towards the end of the 19th century Masonry was regarded in Russia, even in responsible quarters, as a nest of atheistic revolutionaries or as a formidable centre of sinister Jewish organizations plotting against Christianity and lawful governments, incredible as this appears to anyone acquainted with the stabilizing influence which true Masonry exercises in every country, and with the nature of its peaceful and charitable aspirations!

There is ground for belief that in remote Russian provinces, particularly so in the west, Lodges resumed their work soon after the dissolving decree, and continued it, secretly, through the whole of the 19th century. The following Lodges are said to have been working in the Ukraine: The Lodge of Love of Truth, in Poltava; Immortality, in Kiev; Darkness Dispersed, in Gitomir; Osiris, in Kamenez; and Pont Euxin, in Odessa. They all reopened their work, in secrecy, not long after the prohibition of Masonry, and, although working independently, always kept up fraternal relationship.[39]

---

[39] These and further particulars concerning the Ukrainian Masonry are due to Bro. Sitwell and Bro. Shumitzky, both of Paris; the latter an official delegate of Ukrainian Lodges. A real romance of Masonic history is attached to Bro. Shumitzky's arrival at Paris with an important part of Ukrainian Masonic archives; among the papers, brought westward by Bro. Shumitzky, are said to be some valuable French Masonic documents of the 18th century; they were taken into Russia by French refugees, saving themselves and their Masonic treasures from the French revolutionary terror, and now came back to France, saved from the Red Terror in Russia. Truly, history repeats itself!

III.—RUSSIAN FREEMASONRY IN THE 20TH CENTURY.

In 1900 the first Ukrainian Masonic Congress was held; it founded on the 17th January of that year the Grand Lodge of the Ukraine. In 1919, after the establishment of the short-lived independent Ukrainian Republic, the Grand Lodge of the Ukraine officially proclaimed its existence; it united seven principal Lodges, corresponding to seven principal districts of the Ukraine, and is said to have counted then some 6,000 members. The young Grand Lodge entered into fraternal relations with the Grand Orient of Italy, and sent delegates to other countries. The unfortunate advent of the Bolshevist régime forced Ukrainian Lodges to go into retirement once again; still, with commendable courage, they seem to carry on their activities and to adhere to the ancient Masonic landmarks.

In Great Russia, Rosicrucian Lodges, or, better described, private gatherings of Rosicrucians, appear to have continued their secret work even after the Bolshevist revolution; standing far away from every political strife, they worked as before, on the path of moral self-improvement, guided by fundamental Masonic principles of brotherly love, relief, and truth, and culminating their studies in Christian Mysticism.[40]

At the beginning of 1906,[41] some fifteen Russians, well known for their social and political activities, mostly of the " Constitutional-Democratic " party, joined French

---

[40]That there were men in Russia of the 20th century who understood and practised true Masonic principles is testified by a Russian pamphlet, " Who were Russian Masons and what Aims they Pursued? " by Baron A. G. von Kridener, published at Moscow in 1912.

[41]For much of the following information I am indebted to Mr. L. Kandaouroff, of Paris. See A.Q.C., XXXV, p. 291.

Lodges; several became members of the Grand Orient of France, but the majority entered two Lodges working under the Supreme Council of the Ancient and Accepted Scottish Rite—"Kosmos" and "Mount Sinai." On returning to Russia they formed two provisional Lodges: "The Polar Star" in St. Petersburg and "Regeneration" in Moscow. In May, 1908, both Lodges were solemnly opened by two members of the High Council of the Grand Orient, specially sent for that purpose from Paris. At the same time the Grand Lodge of France established two Lodges, one in St. Petersburg,[42] and one in Moscow. Russian Lodges obtained the right to establish further Lodges without interference from Paris, and accordingly, in 1908 and 1909, two more Lodges were opened: "The Iron Ring" in Nijni-Novgorod and one in Kiev.

The existence of Masonic Lodges was discovered by the Russian Government in 1909; it also became known to the authorities that these Lodges were of French origin. The Russian Lodges then resolved to suspend work, and this was adhered to till 1911, when several of their members decided to renew, with all possible prudence, their activities. One could hardly call those activities Masonic, as their chief aim was political—the abolishment of Russian autocracy and the establishment of a democratic régime in the Empire of the Tsar; these members acknowledged allegiance to the Grand Orient of France. Their political organization comprised in 1913-1914 some forty Lodges. In 1915-1916 disagreements arose between their members, who belonged to two political parties, "the Constitutional Democrats" and "the Progressives," and could not agree on a common policy; ten Lodges became dormant, the remaining thirty Lodges[43] continued to work; apparently they took part in the organization of the 1917 March revolution and the establishment of the Provisional Government. Their political object being achieved, the movement began to languish; still, twenty-eight Lodges existed on the eve of the Bolshevist

---

[42]The Phœnix.

[43]It is interesting to note that one of these Lodges consisted exclusively of members of the Douma.

revolution, and since then most of their members have left Russia.

Besides this unfortunate example of a political organization under a Masonic guise, there were in Russia a few English" and Italian Masons. An independent Lodge of the so-called Martinist Rite was formed among the entourage of the Czar, Nicholas II, under the name of " The Cross and the Star "; the Emperor himself is said to have been a member of this lodge, which suspended its work in 1916. Other Martinist Lodges were opened—" Apollonius " in St. Petersburg (1910), " St. John " in Moscow (1911), and " St. Andrew " in Kiev (1912). A very curious Lodge existed among the Russian Navy League; its members called themselves " Philalètes," and, besides serious philanthropic and intellectual work, attempted to pursue a political aim of a character opposite to the Grand Orient Lodges—namely, to support the Monarchical régime of Nicholas II. Probably, this movement arose in connection with the Paris branch of the Swiss Order of the Chevaliers—Philalètes, which established at St. Petersburg two Lodges : " The Pyramid of the North," and " The Star of the North "; this Order pursued studies of symbolism and mysticism.

The attitude of the Bolsheviki towards Masonry of every kind is well illustrated by the resolution passed during the 4th Congress of the Communist International, which was convened at Moscow in 1922. This resolution requires all Communists, if any, belonging to Masonic Lodges, to sever this connection at once or to leave immediately the Communistic party ; no Communist, who has ever belonged to any Masonic organisation, can be appointed to important posts in the party during two years after such severance of relationship with Freemasonry. This discussion and the resulting resolution might have been provoked not only by the remainder of old Russian Lodges, still lingering, but also by attempts made by certain irregular, so-called " Masonic " Bodies to penetrate into Russia even during the present régime.[45]

"Among these were Knight Templars.

[45]Since then some " Masonic " gatherings in Moscow were raided by the Bolshevist police.

The wide-spread interest in Masonry evinced at present among Russian refugees in Europe must be noted here. Already during the Great War, but especially after the Bolshevist revolution, when there occurred so many opportunities for a number of Russians abroad to come into contact with the orthodox Masonry, their prejudices began to undergo a change; several well-known Russians joined Masonic Lodges in those countries in which the wave of the revolution, having washed them off the storm-beaten Russian ship, brought their battered bodies to rest.

In London, a Russian Masonic Circle, comprising Russian Masons under the obedience of the Grand Lodge of England, was formed in 1924. There are a few isolated Russian Masons in Scandinavian countries, and a Russian Lodge, " The Northern Star," exists in Berlin under the warrant of the Grand Lodge of Three Globes. Russian Masons of orthodox allegiance are to be found in France, and a Lodge working partly in Russian has been formed under the Grand National Lodge of Egypt.

In 1922, at the Congress of Lausanne, the Supreme Council of the Ancient and Accepted Scottish Rite in France was charged to organize the " Scottish Rite " for Russia, and on the 10th February, 1927, a Russian Consistory of the 32nd degree—" Rossia," was opened in Paris. There are some 50 Russians, residing in Paris, who belong to " higher " degrees of the Scottish Rite in France.

Under the obedience of the Grand Lodge of France are four Russian Lodges, counting over 200 members, and nearly 100 Russians belonging to Lodges allied to this organization, are dispersed over different parts of the European Continent.

It is curious to note how old family traditions have been kept up in this renewal of interest towards Masonry— Counts Shuvalov, Princes Lobanov-Rostovsky, and many others of the best Russian families whose ancestors played a prominent rôle in the brilliant days of Russian Masonry, have again their representatives among Masonic ranks.

It is to be hoped that Russian Masonry, when reconstituted, will profit by the lessons of the past, and avoiding many pitfalls presented by Continental Masonry, will follow the only true Masonic road indicated by three unerring sign-posts: Brotherly Love, Relief, and Truth.

In concluding this outline of the changing fortunes of Russian Masonry, one can fitly bring to one's memory the spirited words of a Russian Masonic document, dated the 10th September, 1827, just over one hundred years ago, and addressed to Russian Masons, then working under great difficulties :—

Let us with united strength continue the construction of the walls of that building, the foundation of which had been laid so excellently and firmly by our ancestors: each of us has to hew his own rough ashlar, and at the same time all of us together must prepare also other stones suitable for this edifice; let us establish an alliance of love, fidelity to the Order, open-heartedness and mutual friendship in fulfilling the spirit of Brotherhood, let us leave aside all dissimulation, mistrust, reserve and selfishness; so that all together and each individually we may live especially for God, the Order and our Neighbours.

A SHORT BIBLIOGRAPHICAL NOTE OF ORIGINAL RUSSIAN AUTHORITIES.

Barskov, Ja. L. Correspondence of Moscow Masons of the 18th century. Petrograd, 1915.

Bogdanovich, M. N. History of the reign of the Emperor Alexander I. St. Petersburg, 1871.

Bogolubov, B. N. I. Novikov and his time. Moscow, 1916.

Brotherly Instructions addressed to some Brethren Freemasons. Written by Bro. Seddag (Ely). Moscow, 1784.

Eshevsky, S. B. Complete works. V. III. Moscow, 1870.

Kushelev, E. A. Memorandum concerning Masonic Lodges. Russkaia Starina. 1877. V. XVIII.

Longinov, M. N. Novikov and Moscow Martinists. Moscow, 1867.

Masonry in its Past and Present. Edited by S. P. Melgunov and N. P. Sidorov. 2 v. 1914 and 1915.

Pekarsky, P. B. Supplements to the history of Masonry in Russia in the 18th century. St. Petersburg, 1869.

Puipin, A. N. Russian Masonry in the 18th century and the first quarter of the 19th century. Petrograd, 1916.

Puipin, A. N. Social movement in Russia under Alexander I. St. Petersburg. 4th Edition. 1908.

Sokolovskaia, T. The Chapter of Phœnix.

Sokolovskaia, T. Russian Masonry and its significance in the history of social movement.

Tarassov, E. J. Towards the history of Masonry in Russia. A forgotten Rosicrucian, A. M. Kutosov. St. Petersburg, 1911.

Tukalevsky, V. N. Quest of Russian Masons. St. Petersburg, 1911.

Printed by ODHAMS PRESS Ltd., Long Acre, London, W.C.2.

CPSIA information can be obtained
at www.ICGtesting.com
Printed in the USA
BVOW04s1324080217
475657BV00006B/54/P